Composers in this book :

BACH (1685-1750)

MOZART (1756-1791)

BEETHOVEN (1770-1827)

An explanation of musical terms used in this book

Cantata A story or play set to music to be sung by a chorus, but not acted.

Chamber Music Music suited to a room or small hall, and played by three, four or more players.

Concerto A composition for one or more principal instruments, such as violin, piano, etc., accompanied by an orchestra.

Fugue A composition for a given number of parts or 'voices' which enter successively in imitation of each other.

Masque A musical entertainment which includes acting.

Mass A musical setting of the principal Roman Catholic service.

Minuet A graceful dance in triple time.

Motet A church song of praise or gladness.

Opera A play that is mostly sung, and which has costumes, scenery, acting and music to go with the singing.

Oratorio A composition, usually based on a religious theme, for solo voices, chorus and orchestra, dramatic in character but performed without action, costumes or scenery.

Passion Music about the sufferings and death of Jesus on the Cross.

Prelude A musical introduction to music that follows.

Quartet Music for four voices or instruments.

Serenade Music to be played or sung out of doors at night.

Sonata Composition for one instrument (e.g. piano), or two (e.g. piano and violin), usually with three or four movements.

Symphony An elaborate composition for an orchestra, usually having three or four movements in different rhythms.

Toccata A composition for a keyboard instrument, intended to exhibit the skill of the player.

Trio Music for three voices or instruments.

BOOK 1

Lives of the
GREAT
COMPOSERS

by IAN WOODWARD

with illustrations by
MARTIN AITCHISON

Publishers: Wills & Hepworth Ltd., Loughborough
First published 1969 *Printed in England*

Bach (1685-1750)

It would have been very surprising indeed if Johann Sebastian Bach had become anything but a musician. He was born, at Eisenach, into what was perhaps one of the largest musical families ever known, most of his ancestors and relations being organists, oboists, fiddlers, town pipers and music copyists. Music was part of their lives. Between 1560 and 1871 at least fifty-three members of the Bach family occupied positions as town musicians, though not all of them were talented enough to live solely by music. Often they had to work as bakers, weavers, millers or shoemakers in order to add to the money earned as fiddlers or church organists.

The Bach family were always greatly in need of money. They married early and had large families – Johann Sebastian himself became the father of twenty children. Though most musicians tended to travel widely to other countries, with the exception of Johann Sebastian, the Bachs never seemed to find this necessary or attractive. They were quite content to live their lives as simple, respected citizens in the tiny states of Thuringia, tucked away in one corner of Germany.

No doubt the Bach household was filled with the sound of music, which must have roused Johann Sebastian's curiosity and interest at a very early age.

Johann Sebastian Bach grows up with music.

7214 0230 5

Bach's father, Johann Ambrosius, was the Court musician, and he became the boy's first music teacher. Johann Sebastian's school day began at six o'clock in the morning, and music instruction from his father often continued until late into the evening. His health was not very good, and he was quite often absent from school through illness.

His home had a small garden with its own miniature orchard, and here Johann Sebastian acquired his first love of nature. It was here, too, that he received religious instruction from his mother. Lying quietly on the grass, watching the clouds roll by, the young boy listened attentively to the stories from the Scriptures which his mother read to him. These stories were Bach's earliest religious influence.

These happy days came to an abrupt end soon after his ninth birthday. It was then that his dear mother died, followed less than a year later by his father. Fortunately the eldest brother, Johann Christoph, was able to take care of Bach and another brother. Johann Christoph was the organist at Ohrdruf, a small town thirty miles from Eisenach. There the two boys continued their musical training and enrolled at the local school, where Johann Sebastian became a star pupil.

Bach listens as his mother reads stories from the Scriptures.

Young Bach grew more and more fond of 'making music'. His schooldays at Ohrdruf were frequently spent copying out the works of other composers so he could familiarise himself with their style of writing. Often he re-arranged existing music for completely different instruments.

One day he wanted to copy some pieces of music which his brother had locked away in a cupboard. Luckily the cupboard had a simple wire-grille front through which Bach could just pass his small hand. For the next six months Bach removed one sheet at a time when everyone was asleep, and copied each one by moonlight. Each morning he would replace the sheet, and no one was the wiser!

When he was fifteen it was time for Johann Sebastian to start thinking about earning a living. With a friend he left his brother's home for Lüneburg, about two hundred miles from Ohrdruf, to take up the post of choirboy at the convent of St. Michael. Here he was able to complete his education in church music and, by walking to towns as far away as sixty miles, he managed to hear some of the greatest organists of the day. Before long he was writing music for the organ, though mainly variations on hymn tunes.

Bach removes the sheets of music and copies them by moonlight.

Bach secured his first important job in the neighbouring town of Arnstadt. He was then eighteen and employed as organist and choirmaster of a new church that had just been built there. His duties were to train the church choir and play the organ on Sunday morning from eight until ten, on Thursday morning from seven to nine, and on Monday at prayers.

Since his work in the church took up only a fraction of his time, he was able to spend many hours playing and experimenting at the organ. Bach became a great player and his reputation as a virtuoso spread throughout the tiny princedoms. Music flowed from his pen with ease and speed, including cantatas and toccatas, and, with some difficulty at first, those splendid fugues. His *Easter Cantata* was written for his pupils at Arnstadt.

In 1707, at the age of twenty-two, Bach accepted the post of organist to the Church of St. Blasius in Mühlhausen. Though the conditions there were displeasing to him, he nevertheless managed to compose several fine cantatas. He remained there only a year, and during this time he married his little cousin, Maria Barbara.

Bach practises on the organ.

During the summer of 1708, the Duke of Saxe-Weimar admired Bach's musical gifts and engaged him as organist and concert master. For the first time in his life, Bach was happy in his new post. Here at Weimar he wrote some of his finest organ music, including the great Toccata and Fugue in D minor, and the Prelude and Fugue in D.

The Duke was a cultured man, a patron of the arts and a lover of the organ. He had the idea of arranging a music tournament between Bach and Louis Marchand, the great organist of the Court of King Louis XV of France. One day the French organist happened to overhear Bach practising and, filled with awe and admiration, fled the town before the proposed tournament could be held.

Besides being Court organist, Bach also played in the orchestra, either on the clavichord or the violin. Altogether there were twenty-two musicians in the Duke's orchestra. When he obtained the post of Konzertmeister (concert master) in 1714, Bach was expected to write a monthly cantata, as well as other music for the orchestra and music for special occasions. All this proved invaluable experience for him, and, with the many organ recitals he gave in nearby towns, increased his fame as a musician.

Louis Marchand hears Bach practising and flees the town.

When the post of Kapellmeister (head of all the Court music) fell vacant at Weimar in 1716, Bach was bitterly disappointed that the position was not given to him. When a similar position was offered to him the following year by Prince Leopold of Anhalt-Cöthen, Bach promptly accepted. Leopold was a fine musician and treated his new employee with much affection.

Bach was very happy. His duties were confined solely to chamber music, and he was left with plenty of time in which to compose and travel. He went to Leipzig in the hope of meeting Handel, only to find that he had left on the day of Bach's arrival. Later, when he returned in 1720 from a trip to Carlsbad Spa with the Prince's entourage, he learned that his wife, Maria Barbara, had died. She had been a good wife, having brought seven children into the world, and he missed her very much.

The following year he married again. His wife, Anna Magdalena, was the daughter of a town trumpeter, and she was to bear Bach a further thirteen children. She was a fine singer and a skilled music copyist, copying many of her husband's compositions and even getting the children to help. Bach taught her to play the harpsichord, and in the evenings she often played for her weary husband.

Bach becomes a Kapellmeister.

The years spent at Cöthen, between 1717 and 1723, were musically very rich for Bach. He explored the possibilities of the orchestra, which then was not very advanced, and he wrote the six popular *Brandenburg Concertos* for the music-loving prince. There were also cantatas to be written for special occasions, such as weddings and his patron's birthday, as well as preludes, fugues and sonatas for violin and keyboard. For his son, Wilhelm Friedemann, aged nine, he composed a *Little Book for the Keyboard*.

Had Prince Leopold not married a princess who despised music, Bach might well have spent the rest of his life at Cöthen. As it was, he remained there for only six years. After much hesitation, he applied for the vacant post of Cantor of St. Thomas's School at Leipzig, and was accepted. It was not such an attractive post as the one at Cöthen, as he again had choirboys to train, but he wanted it so that his own children could receive a better education.

Bach's responsibilities were to train the choirboys in two churches, to train the town choir and orchestra, and also to direct the University's Musical Society. He had to contend, too, with interfering Rectors who sometimes forced him to accept their favourites in his choir although they could not sing a note.

Bach unwillingly accepts an unsuitable choirboy.

Although Bach suffered from the continual intrigues of the Church Council at St. Thomas's, the last period of his life was nevertheless well spent. The great cantatas, motets and passions, as well as the profound *Mass in B Minor*, were composed. The *St. Matthew Passion* is among his most enduring works. He also wrote a *Christmas Oratorio*, but Handel's *Messiah* has sinced eclipsed it.

While Bach was alive, it was always as the supreme organist, not the composer, that he was revered. His services were in demand for advising on the construction of new organs, opening newly-built ones and giving recitals. When he visited Potsdam in 1747, the King made him play on all the organs in the city. On his return to Leipzig, the flattered Bach composed *A Musical Offering* for the King.

It has been said that the laborious task of copying out his own music all his life, usually in poor light, caused Bach's sight to fail during the last years. He eventually became totally blind, and died from paralysis in 1750. There was no funeral for the great composer, merely a simple burial in the cemetery of St. John's Church. All that the Church Council said was, "Herr Bach was a great musician, no doubt, but now we want a schoolmaster."

Bach advises an organ builder.

Mozart (1756-1791)

Wolfgang Amadeus Mozart was a remarkable figure in the history of music – an infant prodigy. He was born in 1756, just six years after the death of Bach, in the beautiful old town of Salzburg in the Austrian Alps. His parents, Leopold and Anna Maria, had seven children but only two survived; Maria Anna, known affectionately to the family as 'Nannerl', and Wolfgang, born nearly five years later.

Leopold was employed as a musician in the Court of the powerful Archbishop of Salzburg. His duties included the conducting of the Court orchestra and the composing of music for special occasions. He also taught the harpsichord and violin.

It very soon became obvious that Wolfgang was no ordinary child. He loved doing sums and, if nothing more handy was available, he would work them out on the chairs and tables.

When he was nearly three, he took a great deal of interest in Nannerl's music lessons. Each day, after these were over, and when he was scarcely able to reach the keyboard, he would press down two or three keys together and notice the sounds they produced. Soon he was able to distinguish the slightest variation in the pitch of a violin. Nannerl herself was a child prodigy on the harpsichord.

The three-year-old Mozart shows his interest in music.

Leopold soon realised that he had two children of genius on his hands. He therefore decided to give up his other pupils and devote all his time to his children. Young Mozart was just four when his father took over his education. Besides music and arithmetic, Leopold taught him Latin and German. Wolfgang had no other teacher and he never went to school. By the time he was five he was composing minuets, which his father copied into Nannerl's exercise book.

One day, a year later, Leopold returned home from church with a friend and found Wolfgang at a table, quite engrossed with a quill-pen in hand. "I'm writing a piano concerto," he told his father. Leopold picked up the completed sheets, and smiled. All he could see was a scribble of notes written over innumerable ink-blots. However, after a while he noticed to his surprise that the actual notes were written down correctly and showed many new ideas.

Leopold, a deeply religious man, now felt certain that his son had been sent as a gift from Heaven, and that the world should be allowed to share Wolfgang's unique talents. So in 1762 the Mozart family packed their bags and set off on a grand musical tour of Europe.

Leopold sees his son's first 'Piano Concerto'.

Wolfgang was nearly seven when he arrived to play at the Imperial Castle in Vienna. There, in his smart lilac coat, he delighted the Emperor and Empress with his playing on the violin. Nannerl accompanied him on the harpsichord. Afterwards he asked the Emperor to sing a few notes so that he could improvise a tune from them. Wolfgang enjoyed every minute of these 'games,' and even jumped on the Empress's lap and kissed her on the cheek!

The two Mozart children were now in wide demand in the grand houses and Courts of Holland, Switzerland and Germany. In Paris they played in the Court of Louis XV. Louis had three daughters who were fine musicians, and Wolfgang accompanied one of them on the harpsichord while she sang an Italian song. What was so amazing was that Wolfgang had never before heard the song.

When the two children arrived in London, they were announced as 'Miss Mozart of Eleven and Master Mozart of Seven years of age, Prodigies of Genius.' They enjoyed enormous success, and played several times before King George III and Queen Charlotte. Afterwards they had great fun in the pleasure gardens along the Thames, where there were splendid fountains and coloured lights.

Mozart kisses the Empress.

Life in the great cities of Europe must have made Salzburg seem rather a dull place for Mozart when he arrived back in 1766. Yet he was soon off again for Vienna, where the twelve-year-old prodigy wrote two one-act operas, *La Finta Semplice* and *Bastien and Bastienne*. Leopold and young Mozart then headed for Italy.

As in the previous journeys, they stopped at every city, and by the time they reached Rome, Mozart's fame was widely known. They passed through Verona, Bologna, Milan and Florence. In Rome, they attended a performance of Allegri's *Miserere* in the Sistine Chapel. The great work so haunted Mozart's mind that he spent most of the night writing down the entire score from memory. When the Pope heard of this amazing feat, he made the fourteen-year-old boy a Knight of the Golden Spur.

Everywhere Mozart went he was fêted by the Italians, for whom he wrote three symphonies. His greatest honour came when he was made a Member of the Philharmonic Academy. To achieve this it was necessary to compose several pieces of music in three hours while locked in a room. Mozart needed only half an hour.

The fourteen-year-old Mozart writes from memory the entire score of an oratorio he has heard only once.

In 1771, Mozart was invited to write an entertainment for the wedding of the Archduke Ferdinand of Milan and Princess Maria of Modena. *Ascanio in Alba*, as the masque was called, proved very popular – so different from his next opera, *Lucio Silla*, which was produced in Milan the following year. Mozart, then nearly seventeen, had experienced his first failure. He left for Salzburg soon afterwards and never again returned to Italy.

Next year, Mozart set off for Munich, where he had been commissioned by the Elector of Bavaria to write a comic opera. *La Finta Giardiniera*, first produced in 1775, became an immediate success. It was carnival time in Munich and everyone was in gay spirits, including Mozart, who now had every reason to feel pleased with himself.

Mozart spent most of his twentieth year in Salzburg, composing piano concertos, organ works, masses and the well-known *Haffner Serenade*. However, his father was concerned that Mozart had not yet found a permanent position in the music world. As the harsh new Archbishop would not release Leopold for yet another trip, it was decided that his wife should accompany Mozart on a planned journey to Paris.

Mozart and his mother leave for Paris.

For the journey to Paris, the Mozarts had managed to scrape together enough money to buy their own carriage. On the way they passed through Munich, where the young composer offered his service to the Elector. "Yes, my dear child," he replied, "but I am afraid there is no vacancy." Disappointed, mother and son went on to Augsburg, where Mozart delighted in the famous harpsichords and organs of George Andreas Stein. "I prefer Stein's pianofortes," he writes to his father, "for in whatever way I touch the keys, the tone is always even."

The next stop was Mannheim. Mozart was received by Prince Karl Theodor, whose fine orchestra pleased the composer, particularly as it included his favourite instrument, the clarinet. Yet although the Prince gave him the job of teaching his children, it was obvious that Mozart was not going to receive a permanent post as Court musician.

Among his many friends in Mannheim was a music copyist named Fridolin Weber, who had four daughters. The eldest, Josepha, was later to create the Queen of the Night in Mozart's opera *The Magic Flute*. Mozart fell madly in love with the second daughter, Aloysia, but Leopold was furious and ordered Mozart to leave immediately for Paris – but without Aloysia.

Mozart falls in love with Aloysia.

Icy winds whistled through the narrow cobbled streets of Paris when Mozart and his mother arrived there in March 1778. Yet despite an introduction to an influential household, the French capital offered no prospect of a Court appointment. The only work he composed for the stage was a ballet called *Les Petits Riens*. He also wrote his *Paris Symphony*, which was very well received.

Meanwhile, Mozart's mother became ill. A wealthy friend sent his doctor to attend the ailing woman, but nothing could save her and she died two weeks later. Mozart was alone for the first time in his life. He felt helpless and desperate, especially as Parisians had not yet accepted his talents as a composer. Eventually, on the advice of his father, he returned despondently to Salzburg in September.

Back in Salzburg, Mozart was appointed Court organist, a post he disliked and which he accepted only out of a sense of duty to his father. His joy can be imagined when he was given permission to go to Munich, where he had been invited to write the opera *Idomeneo*. The Archbishop at Salzburg was jealous of Mozart's vast popularity. After a violent quarrel, the Archbishop's friend, the Count of Arco, kicked Mozart out and Mozart left Salzburg for good.

Mozart is kicked out of the Ducal Palace.

Mozart journeyed to Vienna and married one of Weber's daughters, Constance. He was twenty-six and she eighteen. They had a son, Karl. From then on, money was always in short supply, though the couple were very happy. Among Mozart's friends at that time was the composer Haydn, and Mozart dedicated some of his string quartets to him. Altogether this was an important period in Mozart's life, when he poured out some of his greatest symphonies and operas.

The Marriage of Figaro, perhaps his most popular opera, was written in 1786. *Don Giovanni* and *Cosi fan tutte* followed. After the death of Gluck, Mozart was appointed Court Composer, but at only a third of the previous man's salary. He began to get deeper in debt.

While he was at work on *The Magic Flute* in 1791, he was visited by a mysterious stranger, dressed in a dark cloak, who commissioned a *Requiem Mass* (special funeral music) for a patron whose name he could not disclose. Though Mozart was then desperately ill, he set to work on the *Requiem*. He was a superstitious man, and feared that he was writing his own *Requiem*. This proved to be so, for he died of typhus before he was able to finish it. A few days later, Wolfgang Amadeus Mozart was buried in a pauper's grave.

A mysterious stranger calls on Mozart.

Beethoven (1770-1827)

Ludwig van Beethoven is today regarded as the Shakespeare of music. Appropriately he once referred to himself as a 'tone-poet'. He was born in Bonn, in the heart of Germany's lovely Rhineland and, like Bach and Mozart before him, came from a musical family. Both his father and grandfather were employed as musicians in the Court of the Elector in Bonn, though the Beethoven family originally came from Belgium.

Ludwig's father, Johann, a singer in the Elector's chapel, was married in 1767 to Maria Magdalena, a kind-hearted if not very educated woman. Of their seven children, only three survived – Ludwig, born in 1770, being the first, and two younger boys, Kaspar Anton Karl and Nikolaus Johann.

Johann van Beethoven was a weak man, fond of drink, and often severe with young Ludwig for not taking an interest in music. Ludwig could be headstrong and obstinate, and sometimes he could be neither bullied nor coaxed into playing another note at his music lessons, which in any case he would make every possible excuse to avoid.

He was an intelligent, sensitive, shy little boy, who nevertheless got up to all the usual pranks. Apart from the difficulties with his father over his music lessons, his early life was serene and happy, his mother was kind, and the maid would take him for long walks in the beautiful countryside, or in the magnificent Palace gardens.

Young Ludwig tries to avoid his music lesson.

Young Beethoven went to the local school, trotting along with his slate and books with other children, and quickly learning to read and write. He also mastered Latin at great speed, and enough French to write it intelligibly.

His father became ambitious for him, no doubt inspired by the triumphs of the child-prodigy Mozart, which were then well-known in the Rhineland. Johann must have hoped his own son might win equal fame. However, Ludwig's talents as a musician were not the kind that blossom at an early age. All the same, his father tried hard with Ludwig, and presented him in a public concert when he was only eight, though advertising the boy as six. One wonders how many of the audience were deceived!

Schooldays finished for Ludwig when he was eleven, and at last his interest in music came to life. After a brief visit to Holland with his mother, he settled down to a purely musical education. His tutor was Christian Gottlob Neefe, the new Court Organist at Bonn. Neefe was a poet as well as musician. He had numerous acquaintances in the musical and intellectual world, and this noble and cultured man introduced his young pupil to a whole world of new ideas and thoughts that were not possible in his own rather ordinary home. Beethoven the artist was born.

Ludwig progressed so well that within two years he published his Three Trios, and was appointed assistant organist to Neefe.

LUDWIG
VAN
BEETHOVEN

6
Jahren

The next few years were very happy for Beethoven. Bonn acquired a new Elector, Maxmilian Franz, who did all he could to encourage the Arts, opening debating clubs, musical and literary societies. The young musician kept his eyes and ears open so that he could learn as much as possible, and mature both in personality and musicianship. He taught music to children of rich homes, and his appearance gained him the nickname of 'the Spaniard'.

Beethoven was nearly seventeen when he made his first visit to Vienna. He had by then received a thorough grounding in composition from Neefe, had written some promising works, and was an accomplished pianist. In Vienna he hoped to study under the famed Mozart. Yet although Mozart was greatly impressed by Beethoven's skill at improvising on the piano, the proposed lessons were shattered by the news that Ludwig's mother was seriously ill. Beethoven arrived home just in time and was at his beloved mother's side when she died.

The heavy responsibility of looking after the family now fell squarely on Beethoven's shoulders. His father's drunkenness had become progressively worse, and so had his voice, and he was eventually dismissed from the Elector's service. Now, at eighteen, Beethoven was drawing a larger salary, all of which he needed to feed his father and two brothers.

Beethoven plays to Mozart in Vienna.

Christmas 1790 was a time Beethoven never forgot, for he then had his first meeting with the great composer Haydn, who was passing through Bonn on his way to London. Even more exciting was that two of Beethoven's closest friends, the rich Count Waldstein and Stephen von Breuning, were planning to send him on a second trip to Vienna. This time he was to receive lessons in counterpoint from Haydn.

Vienna, the great musical city of Mozart and Haydn, immediately captured Beethoven's affection. From the moment he arrived there in 1792, he knew it was the city of his dreams. There he stayed for the rest of his life, his father having died soon after he left Bonn.

The planned lessons with Haydn were not very successful. Their different temperaments were quite unsuited to one another, though this never led to any quarrels. Haydn, kindly and courteous, must have found the boorish, self-willed behaviour of his pupil quite contrary to his liking. Beethoven, on his part, felt that he was not progressing sufficiently under the old man's care. Because of this, he had been taking lessons secretly from two other teachers, Schenk and Albrechtsberger. After 1795, he taught himself.

Beethoven disagrees with his teacher, Haydn.

At twenty-six, Beethoven was now enjoying one of the happiest periods in his life. He was popular in the houses of the rich, he enjoyed the company of many influential friends, and he had his own apartment in the house of one of his greatest admirers, Prince Lichnowsky. There were garden parties in the afternoons, followed in the evenings by musical parties. Beethoven was always the life and soul of the party. He delighted everyone with his improvisations on the piano, while embarrassing some with his arrogance and bad manners.

During this time it was Beethoven the pianist, not the composer, who was in such demand. Frequent concert tours were made to Prague, Berlin, Dresden and Nuremberg, though the planned visits to Paris and London came to nothing. He was now regarded as one of the greatest pianists in Vienna.

Beethoven was always passionately fond of nature. He spent many long holidays in the country, where he took frequent walks. There was always a notebook in his pocket for scribbling down ideas that came to him. It was this love of the countryside that inspired him to write his famous *Pastoral Symphony*, where, if you listen carefully, you can hear the singing of birds, a tumbling waterfall and gambolling lambs. Even if you are not listening carefully, you cannot miss the magnificent thunderstorm when it comes in the fourth movement.

Beethoven makes notes in the countryside.

The year 1800 marked a turning point in Beethoven's career. His fame as a composer was now beginning to dwarf even his genius on the keyboard, but at this time Beethoven had cause for great concern, for he found that he was gradually losing his hearing. He was most anxious that no-one should know of his complaint, for he feared that this knowledge might lose him work.

Always sensitive, he began to withdraw from society. Unable to hear more than snatches of conversation, he grew suspicious, often imagining people were plotting against him. Some brief relief of his suffering was brought by a girl of seventeen, the Countess Giulietta Guicciardi, with whom he was in love and to whom he dedicated what is now known as the *Moonlight Sonata*. The courtship was short, for she married someone else the following year.

By 1802, Beethoven's deafness was known to most people. This, as well as the Countess's marriage, preyed heavily on his mind until he could bear it no longer. He retreated to the country where he wrote the famous "Heiligenstadt Testament", which tells how intolerable he found life. He contemplated suicide, but rejected the thought . . . "despite all Nature's obstacles, I shall have done everything in my power to become a worthwhile artist and an honourable man . . ." he wrote.

Beethoven realizes that he is becoming deaf.

Beethoven returned to Vienna and seemed charged with a new vitality. He became a great admirer of Napoleon Bonaparte, whom he regarded as a liberator of the ordinary people. For his hero he wrote the vast Symphony No. 3, *The Eroica*, but when, in 1804, Napoleon proclaimed himself Emperor of France, Beethoven's disappointment was so great ("he is only mortal, like the rest of us", he said) that he angrily scribbled out the name Napoleon from the title page. Instead he wrote simply, "To the memory of a great man".

Deafness was now becoming more and more severe, and by the time he was forty conversation was only possible by writing messages in a little notebook. Dozens of these 'conversation books' remain. He was subject to bitter moods, and often behaved very badly to the very people who admired him most. Nevertheless many friends remained loyal to him. Among them was Goethe, the great poet, with whom he went for long country walks.

What a picture he must have presented to the rare (and courageous) pupil who came to his room. From his ears stuck out pieces of cotton wool which had been dipped in some yellow fluid in the eternal hope of a cure. Books, manuscripts and clothes – and often the remains of an earlier meal – were scattered all around.

Between the years 1812 and 1817, very little music was provided by the composer who was yet to write the great *Choral Symphony*.

The deaf Beethoven in his untidy room.

However, shut away in a silent world, Beethoven was experimenting boldly with music, and his work was years in advance of his times. Many found it incomprehensibly 'modern'. Indeed his later works were not fully appreciated for almost a century. However, his last great Symphony, the 9th, known as the *Choral* because he used singers as well as orchestra, received a great ovation at its first playing. Beethoven, who was standing in the orchestra pit, had to be turned round by one of the players to *see* the applause which he could not hear.

Beethoven became a recluse and shunned people almost entirely. At the end of 1826 he was in poor health and went to stay with his high and mighty brother, Nicolaus Johann, who had made a fortune as an apothecary. Beethoven was on very bad terms with his brother's wife, and perhaps it was her fault that at the end of his stay his health was no better. He was refused the use of the family carriage and was sent off in the milk waggon.

Beethoven returned to Vienna a sick man. He took to his bed but even there started planning future compositions. However, after rallying for three months he died in the midst of a tremendous thunderstorm on the evening of March 26th, 1827, surrounded by close friends and presents from admirers.

Beethoven, a sick man, leaves his brother's home in a milk waggon.

Well-known pieces by the Composers in this book

BACH

The Brandenburg Concertos

Six concertos for various groups of instruments, perhaps the most popular of Bach's instrumental works.

Suite No. 3 in D

This suite contains the slow melody known as the *Air on the G string*.

The Well-Tempered Clavier

Sometimes called the "Old Testament of Music". Forty-eight preludes and fugues with two in each of the musical keys. Gounod turned Prelude No. 1 in C major into his popular *Ave Maria*.

Toccato and Fugue in D minor

The best known of Bach's fine organ works. Orchestral arrangements have been made and Walt Disney uses the piece in his film *Fantasia*.

St. Matthew Passion

Bach's greatest religious masterpiece which, like Handel's *Messiah*, has become an annual event in many places.

MOZART

Symphony No. 39 in E flat Major
Symphony No. 40 in G minor
Symphony No. 41 in C major (Jupiter)

These symphonies contain some of the most perfect music ever written. They were all composed in a six week period and within three years of Mozart's early death.

Eine kleine Nachtmusik *(A little Night Music)*

This serenade for strings has become one of the world's most popular pieces.

The Ladybird Key Words Reading Scheme is based on these commonly used words. Those used most often in the English language are introduced first—with other words of popular appeal to children. All the Key Words list is covered in the early books, and the later titles use further word lists to develop full reading fluency. The total number of different words which will be learned in the complete reading scheme is nearly two thousand. The gradual introduction of these words, frequent repetition and complete 'carry-over' from book to book, will ensure rapid learning.

The full-colour illustrations have been designed to create a desirable attitude towards learning— by making every child *eager* to read each title. Thus this attractive reading scheme embraces not only the latest findings in word frequency, but also the natural interests and activities of happy children.

Each book contains a list of the new words introduced.

W. MURRAY, the author of the Ladybird Key Words Reading Scheme, is an experienced headmaster, author and lecturer on the teaching of reading. He is co-author, with J. McNally, of 'Key Words to Literacy'—a teacher's book published by The Schoolmaster Publishing Co. Ltd.

THE LADYBIRD KEY WORDS READING SCHEME has 12 graded books in each of its three series—'a', 'b' and 'c'. As explained in the handbook 'Teaching Reading', these 36 graded books are all written on a controlled vocabulary, and take the learner from the earliest stages of reading to reading fluency.

The 'a' series gradually introduces and repeats new words. The parallel 'b' series gives the needed further repetition of these words at each stage, but in different context and with different illustrations.

The 'c' series is also parallel to the 'a' series, and supplies the necessary link with writing and phonic training.

An illustrated booklet—'Notes for Teachers'—can be obtained free from the publishers. This booklet fully explains the Key Words principle and the Ladybird Key Words Reading Scheme. It also includes information on the reading books, work books and apparatus available, and such details as the vocabulary loading and reading ages of all books.